Nada

MISDIAGNOSED
RESTORED BY RHYTHMS OF GRACE

Copyright © 2013 by Nada B. Owusu M.D.

Misdiagnosed
Restored by Rhythms of Grace
by Nada B. Owusu M.D.

Printed in the United States of America

ISBN 9781628711288

All rights reserved solely by the author. The author guarantees all contents are original and do not infringe upon the legal rights of any other person or work. No part of this book may be reproduced in any form without the permission of the author. The views expressed in this book are not necessarily those of the publisher.

Unless otherwise noted, scripture quotations are from the Holy Bible; New International Version (NIV).Copyright © 1973, 1978, 1984 by Zondervan.

Scripture quotations marked Amplified are taken from The Amplified Bible. Copyright 1965 by Zondervan Publishing House.

www.xulonpress.com

Dedication

This book is dedicated to my three wonderful children, Andrew, Joseph and Krystal. It is an honor to be called your mother. The name "mommy" is the second sweetest sound in my ears after the name of Jesus.

My earnest prayer is that you will remain receptive to the things of God and enjoy the unforced rhythms of His grace and love. May you explore your God-inspired potentials, fulfill your destinies, experience His abundant life, live victoriously and bless mankind.

To my nieces and nephews, Auntie Nada wrote this for you too, and I am confident that God will do exceedingly above what I have asked for you in prayer.

Acknowledgements

The inspiration for this book and everything I do comes from none other than my Heavenly Father. My goal in life is to reflect the glorious beauty of His dear Son, walk in the power of His Spirit and to unashamedly proclaim His gospel. I am eternally grateful for all that He has imparted to me and I understand that "to whom much is given, much is expected."

To Victor, my handsome prince, my gentle lion and the love of my life, the security of your love propels me to soar and motivates me for projects like this.

To my special treasures, Andrew, Joseph and Krystal, thank you for enriching my life with your humor, laughter and your unique personalities.

To my dearest friend and the leader of my cheer-leading squad, Pastor Sharon Motley, Thank you for believing in this project and for your constant reminders.

To my god-daughter, Stephanie Taylor, thank you for taking time out of your very busy schedule to edit this work. You have been gifted and appointed for such a time as this.

To my dearest brother and friend, Apostle Michael Baah-Yeboah, your fervent prayers are availing much.

Lastly, to all my friends and prayer partners, thank you for being co-laborers in the kingdom of our Lord and King.

Introduction

This book definitely forced me outside my comfort zone. I like to write, but fiction was not something I felt qualified to do.

As a mother I have watched several movies with my children that were not exactly what the rating suggested.

I kept telling them that one day they will go to the movies and the writer will be none other than their own mother.

Of course they all laughed and before long I joined in the laughter and threw away the idea.

Several years passed and suddenly one day while on my lunch break, God birthed this beautiful story line in me. I was amazed to see how well He blended my passion for medicine and the gospel and even spiced it with some traditional African practices.

A few friends have asked if this is a true story because of how real the characters appear.

We all have a story to tell and this could easily be mine except for the fact I didn't grow up with a silver spoon and a private jet.

However, I also had a very loving father who believed in my limitless potential and adored me till his recent transition to heaven at the age of 102.

My father believed I could be the first doctor in my family. From the tender age of 5, I was consumed with this passion of becoming a doctor. I had no other interests until my second year in Medical school when I fell in love with Jesus. He took me on this exciting journey of more than enough, and expanded my passions to include singing, song-writing, evangelism, teaching and writing.

Enough about me, because this is not my personal story but a love story that evolves out of the ashes of prejudice.

Prejudice has no respect of nationality, race, color, gender, profession, social class, religious beliefs or Christian denomination. Like a hurricane, it leaves its victims with emotional, mental distress and missed opportunities.

Think about the friendships and relationships we failed to build because of prejudice. Well, the characters in this story lost opportunities too but God in His infinite wisdom found a way to heal them and even use their enemies to bless them.

This piece is truly fictional but it is laced with layers of God's grace and love that has the power to transform you.

So relax and see how the unforced rhythms of God's grace enriched the lives of the characters in ***Misdiagnosed***.

HARVARD LAW SCHOOL GRADUATION CEREMONY

Parents, family, and loved ones arrived at Harvard University with such anticipation and pride to witness the graduation of their loved ones from its law school. The atmosphere was filled with excitement and all the Ivy League bells and whistles necessary for a prestigious law school graduation. Mr. Wood, an alumnus of the school arrived in style on his private jet with his family to celebrate the graduation of Krystal, his only daughter. Krystal was the epitome of effortless pulchritude. She preferred academics to the fashion runways of Milan and New York that her peers obsessed over. Her late grandfather used to say, "King Solomon must be so sorry for not meeting you- because your beauty would have inspired him to write many more love songs". No one who encountered her failed to notice her almond eyes, which were so captivating above her radiant smile showing teeth so flawless that, if they were contagious, orthodontics would find themselves bankrupt with nothing to fix.

Krystal's family took more than their allotted share of seats due to every living member of the family being present, including her "boyfriend". They had broken up so many times that no one knew how to define their relationship, but needless to say, he was also in attendance.

Krystal was very popular with the school's faculty and her classmates as evidenced by the ovation and accolades she received for her achievements. Law was like second nature for her, having grown up around her father's big law firm. She spent most summers as an intern filing and typing documents, and even had the privilege of sitting in on some court cases.

Following Krystal's commencement ceremony a professor, who was her father's roommate and good friend, hosted the family at his residence. It was a beautiful reception with a gourmet chef serving a large selection of hor d'oeuvres.

Her dad was beaming with so much pride it was infectious. Now his dream of having his daughter take over his firm was one step closer to coming true. Ironically, law was the first thing Krystal was exposed to, but the last profession she truly wanted. She wanted to be a doctor at one time, and spent a year at Georgetown University as a medical student. Medicine had always intrigued Krystal. She was an expert of television medicine and was ready for the challenge in real life, but she was quickly talked out of medical school and never looked back.

Harvard Law School Graduation Ceremony

The family shared many stories of her childhood and had a great time at the party in her honor. Soon it was time to return to Maryland and everyone hurried to avoid missing a late night flight. Everyone extended his or her goodbyes and thanked everyone once more for coming, before heading home.

The family continued the celebration on the jet, snacking and sharing many more funny memories. Krystal enjoyed most of the stories but her parents noticed that several times she had a blank stare in the middle of conversations revolving around topics that she usually had strong opinions on. Krystal was busy wondering what her life would be like if this had this been her graduation from medical school. That thought always nauseated her. It was the same feeling she had on her last day in anatomy class. She battled with her imagination, convincing herself that her life as a medical student could not compare to her triumphs in Law school. She never went into much detail about her decision to leave Georgetown because she feared her father's reaction, if he knew the truth. His influence with the faculty could have brought painful consequences to those who caused her such pain. Her mother knew just by looking into her eyes the day she came home from medical school that her daughter had endured a devastating blow.

Her mother was naturally surprised when Krystal mentioned her desire to attend the upcoming graduation of her former classmates from Georgetown medical school. Krystal had no intention of going when her only true friend from Georgetown, Tamara Hale, sent her an invitation. The timing was wrong, overlapping with her family's vacation to the Atlantis in the Bahamas, and overall she just didn't care. Somehow after celebrating her own graduation, she suddenly became distracted with thought of her former Georgetown classmates' graduation. She asked if her mother could change their travel dates to enable her to attend the ceremony at Georgetown. Her mother was a bit offended that she was more concerned about that ceremony than acknowledging all the effort taken to plan this special vacation for her.

"Which other class are you referring to?" her mother inquired.

"My medical school class is graduating in two weeks," Krystal answered.

"Wow, I didn't realize you kept in contact with them. That is very impressive. Doctors are useful friends to have."

Her mother was not as impressed as she sounded, because she whispered to herself, "I thought those were the same people who practically drove you out of medicine. It seems like you can't even tell your friends from your enemies."

Krystal heard her clearly, because she rolled her huge, slanted eyes, and adjusted her seat for more comfort. Her mother being the wise woman that she is suggested the family watch a movie to maintain the celebratory mood.

The truth was that Krystal barely stayed in contact with her few medical school friends, so this sudden obsession over their graduation was a real concern for her mother. Krystal even wondered about her unusual sudden interest. Was it to say a final goodbye to a profession she still admired, or was it so say a proper farewell to her few friends before they moved on in pursuit of their individual specialties? Could it be that she wanted to flaunt her success in law school to a few of her enemies who **misdiagnosed** her?

She had a grin on her face as she processed all of these thoughts. She was about to confront some young doctors about making a wrong diagnosis, and perhaps even playfully threaten to sue them for defamation. Her expression indicated that she wanted to make one last impression on her former classmates. She fell asleep in the middle of mentally plotting her revenge.

The plane ride was even shorter than usual because she slept the rest of the flight, having vivid dreams of her life as a medical student.

Georgetown Medical School

Krystal's dream was about her life in Georgetown, beginning on the day of orientation as a medical student. She arrived late to the auditorium in her flashy designer suit, drawing attention and admiration from a few male students. Her clothing was exclusive, her shoes were one-of-a kind and her jewelry made them stutter.

"Who does she think she is — a model?" A classmate whispered.

Before they could reach a conclusion, the Dean of the school of medicine shouted, "Nice to see you Krystal. I am so glad you followed my advice to become a Doctor instead of a Lawyer," He beamed with malicious joy as he spoke to her and even stepped down from the lecture platform, walked to her seat, held out his hand to shake hers. "I will share my thoughts on your first day with your father at the next board meeting." He said with laughter, referring to her tardiness. The auditorium was so silent you could hear a pin drop.

Wow! That personal acknowledgement from the Dean immediately set her apart from the rest of the class. That was not fair at all, and after that nobody made the effort to truly know who she really was. Most of them labeled her as a snob because they felt she got special treatment, which they thought was undeserved.

They said to each other, "Wonder how special it will feel to have the dean beg you to attend his school."

Others thought, "Hope she didn't come through the back door. After all, her dad sits on the hospital board."

Regardless, they did not approve of her tardiness and were disappointed that instead of being reprimanded, she was hailed like a hero.

They assumed many things, judged her and sentenced her to her own unique class of "medically dumb," like the movie, "Legally Blonde."

How could they label her from one instance like that? How does one have to look to be considered intelligent?

Krystal was dealt a fortunate hand in life, which unfortunately backfired through her enduring alienation from those around her.

Her spotless silver spoon has repelled almost everyone from embracing the person she only wishes they could see.

One can only imagine how upset she was when she later found out what was being said about her.

These were supposed to be student doctors. Medical students who were being taught how to take a good medical history, examine their subject, and order some laboratory tests or even some diagnostic radiological studies before making a diagnosis.

No, they did otherwise. They took one look at her, and misdiagnosed her.

Then they poisoned her with their toxic medicine, because the diagnosis was wrong, the therapy was bound to be wrong.

How could they possibly call her "medically dumb," She had the same right to be there as all of them. She was the valedictorian of her high school class like most of them were and her MCAT score for medical school was in the top 20% of the nation ,but nobody knew all that except the admission board. Krystal actually took the LSAT for law school as well because she was torn between the two professions and did equally well.

The "dumb" part really bothered her when she found out. She ended up being one of the smartest ones in the class. Nicholas, a classmate said jokingly, "Wow you made a fool of us because some of us had coined you "medically dumb". When Krystal asked him why he thought she wouldn't be smart, his answer was, "forgive me but I thought you spent so much time on being a "fashionista" that there would be much less time for your course work. He was surprised about how well Krystal took his comment and even more amazed when she went on to say she had been a tomboy until her last 2 years in high school when her mother took an active role on what she wore. Nicholas must have really enjoyed talking to her because he invited her to join his study group. His girlfriend Tamara was a member of the study group, and she and Krystal ended up being great friends.

As her study group got better acquainted with her, they were able to correct some of the misconceptions about her academic potential. They obviously couldn't convince everyone else of her photographic memory and strong study ethics because some still assumed that the entire faculty was giving her special treatment.

They assumed that the entire faculty knew about her father's position on the hospital board but that was far from true. The only conversation some of these students made with her was when they made unfair remarks like, "Have you ever considered modeling or even business/law, like your dad?" She always had a nice answer for them. Once she answered "Oh pardon me, but I thought I could do it all, fashion, medicine and law."

When it came time for their anatomy rotation her class was divided into three major alphabetic groups and she ended up in the last group .This group comprised of people with last names starting with S through to Z. So since her last name was Wood she found herself in the same group as Quarmaine Smith, better known as Q.

Quarmaine himself was not popular in the class either, because he was considered overweening by many. He was also not impressed with Krystal's academic performance or her father's position. He got the highest mark on most of their quizzes and tests except on occasion when Krystal took that spot. Even when he scored higher, it was only a point or two from Krystal. Tamara always told Krystal that Q was egotistic and just couldn't accept the fact that a girl, Krystal in particular, could be as smart as he.

He spent every free second studying and wouldn't even join in class jokes or any non academic conversations. He dominated their academic discussions and made a point to always quote several articles to prove a simple point. He was one of those who assumed Krystal was getting special treatments and on few occasions, challenged her to live up to the expectation of the medical profession. Those expectations were the strict ones that he had imposed on himself. They had several unpleasant encounters.

One notable scene was in the anatomy laboratory, when their group had to dissect a cadaver's nervous system. Krystal refused to participate — at least, that was Q's version — and he accused her of making his team fall behind. Q did most of the dissecting, all the while raining insults on her and fuming with rage. The other team members felt very uncomfortable with his behavior but unfortunately nobody stopped him. Q's comments were sharper than the scalpel he held, and with every incision she bled within. Q could turn any simple "non academic" conversation again into a Krystal bashing session.

At the beginning of the session Krystal's nails tore through the gloves as she attempted to put them on revealing her well manicured French tips. The entire group laughed at her with the exception of Q who didn't think it was funny to have sharp nails as a medical student period. He mocked her for coming into the dissection lab totally unprepared to participate, knowing very well that those well-manicured nails would interfere with proper handling of the scalpel.

Krystal explained that she normally doesn't get her nails that long but she was in a wedding that weekend and didn't have time to remove them that morning. Q was not interested in anything she had to say. Q had no idea how hard the practical aspect of anatomy, especially this dissecting of cadavers was for her, and how it had made her reconsider law school. She had asked God for a sign as to whether to continue with medicine or switch to law but she was not expecting an answer so soon.

The teaching assistant ignored the commotion, intentionally walking away when Krystal started to cry silently. She looked sternly into Q's eyes and said "enough is enough Q, you may have a point today, but you do not have the last word on my destiny. I don't know what your problem is but I hate to have even my enemies consider you their doctor one day. I hope you never graduate from here because a bitter doctor is always a dangerous doctor." In addition to her encounter with Q, the smell of the formaldehyde- the basic ingredient in conventional embalming fluid, made her nauseous, and the sight of all those cadavers sent chills down her spine.

She walked out that day in tears, but what she really wanted to do was scream, throw a tantrum, or even cut Q with her scalpel. Instead, she controlled all those toxic feelings, but her tears were uncontrollable. She knew as she walked out of that class that there was no turning back. It was common for medical students to have meltdowns in their first year but for Krystal this was an unusual answer to her questions about the profession.

Her few faithful friends, led by Tamara, consoled her as best they could and even people she considered enemies were very sympathetic- but she was resolute. The circumstances were unpleasant, but God used them to push her into her destiny and His divine purpose. When she left the campus, she drove straight to her paternal grandmother's house and wept like a baby on her huge shoulders as she had on many occasions in the past. She ended up spending the night after a long prayerful discussion of the encounter and how it played in God's plan for her life. She left her grandmother's house with so much peace, and as they had discussed she convinced her parents to give her time to search her soul and evaluate her choices well. Her father, the famous lawyer Woods was secretly happy about the possibility of her choosing law over medicine but he did his best not to influence her decision. Because of his own bias towards law he also did not use his position on the hospital board either.

She visited several law schools but was very captivated by Harvard for so many great reasons and was so excited when she transferred there the following academic year.

Life is never easy, but much more bearable when people find themselves in the center of their purpose. That was exactly what Krystal experienced in law school. She was very passionate about the whole experience, and therefore she blossomed and excelled.

Krystal could never forget the humiliating remarks Q made towards her. It made no sense to her – what did she do to Q and the other boys? She had always been admired by boys, but no one had ever made her feel as inferior as Q did that day.

Q, an Aspiring Doctor

Q was considered the exception by his colleagues. He seemed to have no regard or respect for any of his classmates. He considered most of them too privileged or less intelligent. He was an ambitious man who was extremely focused on becoming an excellent doctor. His main concern was to impress his professors and make wise use of every second to stay in the top 5% of the class. Medicine was going to be his ticket to a better and stable socioeconomic status for his family. Walking the corridors of the hospital in his white coats always gave him a sense of pride in his accomplishments.

He was without a doubt the best in his class, and was acknowledged for his achievements by his professors. However, his frequent outbursts of anger and arrogant attitude toward his classmates isolated him from his peers. With time, he became more and more controversial, always trying to debate simple and basic medical theories or quoting the latest article in the New England Journal of Medicine to impress. He kept people at arm's length and never socialized on campus. To tell the truth, he just could not afford it.

Q was not proud of his current socio-economic class, which was much lower than what he enjoyed when his father was alive. It was much easier to avoid his peers than open up his wounds to them. His father was actually an alumnus of Georgetown. He played basketball and upon graduation spent 2 years playing professional basketball in Italy before joining an NBA team in Atlanta. His parents were high school sweethearts. They married during his second year of college and within 2 years they had two handsome boys. His mother withdrew from nursing school and became a full time mother and wife to her growing family. They lived the fast life drove the best cars and spent their fortune unwisely without investing. His father's career ended abruptly after a motor vehicle accident under the influence of alcohol left him incapacitated. After several months of rehabilitation and physical therapy he took a coaching position at one of the high schools in Washington D.C. They still had a fairly decent life until diabetes, depression and alcoholism left him unemployed for many years. At the time of his death he had moved the family back to his parent's home in D.C and even though the home was decent, the neighborhood had gone through major changes.

The faculty and his colleagues finally got a little insight into his mysterious life and struggles when both his mother and brother became patients in the ICU one day. His brother had developed kidney failure because of his poorly controlled Type One Diabetes Mellitus. He needed dialysis urgently, but while waiting in the ER, his mother suffered a mild stroke from malignant hypertension complicated by intracerebral hemorrhage.

These two were the only family he had. They were the reason he was working so hard. He needed them to live so he could also have a reason for living. It was extremely difficult balancing the dual acts of a caregiver and a medical student in the same institute. Q became more and more exhausted, emotionally, mentally, and physically. He hit his lowest point when he broke down in the ICU one day, weeping uncontrollably. His colleagues and professors looked on, not knowing how to comfort the "bad boy," who, as they learned later, was only a boy with a badly broken heart.

Tears that he had held back for years poured like a fountain on the floor. It was at that point that Dr. Akita, a visiting professor from Ghana, embraced him in her loving arms and prayed softly over him. Her prayers for him were answered, because both his mother and brother made good progress and were discharged from the hospital in two weeks.

Dr. Akita took a special interest in Q after their encounter in the ICU, inviting him over to her apartment many times for some of her delicious African meals (fried plantain, beans, jollof rice, goat meat, peanut butter soup, and other delicacies). She also used that opportunity to minister to him and almost led him to Christ. As he opened up more to her, she made him aware that he must learn to turn everything over to his Creator or he would end up with a mental breakdown. She gave him some good books to read and made him promise to see the school counselor and therapist regularly.

Tamara, Krystal's friend and other Christians in his class started reaching out to him. The counseling and family therapy helped him to be more optimistic and more relaxed. His attitude really got better, he started smiling and displayed a charming sense of humor, but then misfortune overtook him again.

He was summoned to the Dean's office one fine afternoon and questioned over several controlled prescriptions his brother may have written in his name. The Dean believed his story because he had a good academic reputation and excellent work ethic. Most of the medications were misspelled and contraindicated in renal failure, his brother's medical condition.

Q stormed out of the Dean's office in great fury, forgetting to sign off his patients to the "on call" doctor. He went straight home to confront his brother.

Unfortunately, that was the last time his colleagues saw him.

Just like the saying, "life came at him fast." One day he was an aspiring final year medical student, and the next day he was in a prison awaiting trial for possession of cocaine with intent to distribute.

What could have happened? That was the question his classmates had in mind as they anticipated their upcoming graduation.

GEORGETOWN MEDICAL SCHOOL GRADUATION CEREMONY

It was a beautiful day in Washington, DC, as family and friends took their seats on the lawn to witness the graduation of their loved ones from Georgetown Medical School.

Krystal and Adele, her "cousin" and personal hairdresser, arrived fashionably late for the graduation ceremony in her mother's new Mercedes, planning to make one last impression on her former classmates. She was unusually nervous, displaying more anxiety than excitement. After all, this would have been her own graduation, had she not transferred to law school.

Fortunately her designer shades hid her empty eyes and hurting soul.

As she walked the same grounds she fled from years ago, Krystal relived some of her experiences in Georgetown. She remembered how, despite her high IQ, her stunning beauty and flare for fashion — compounded by having a rich and powerful daddy — made her easy and convenient target for prejudice. She also remembered the few but dearest friends she had made.

Her favorite one was of course Tamara Hale, a beautiful soul and a true Christian, one who fit the description of a "friend who sticks closer than a brother." The thought of reuniting with Tamara warmed her heart, but that feeling was short-lived. The mere possibility of coming face to face with Q made her sick; she had no idea this was highly unlikely.

"I hope you never graduate from medical school. After all, who would ever want to see a doctor with such a ghetto name?" That was the last statement she made to Q.

What would she say to him now,"congratulations Dr Q" and how would he respond?

The more she thought about their encounter at the anatomy lab the more she regretted the idea of going to the ceremony.

She turned to Adele, and said, "Perhaps coming here was not such a good idea. It is bringing up some chilling memories. Let's just go home."

She didn't share her notion at all. "No, no, no, no way, not after you got me dressed up like some aristocrat, having me memorize all these eloquent greetings and compliments like, 'What a lovely day,' 'Pleasure to meet you, ma'am,' 'You must be very proud of your baby,' 'What medical specialty are you planning to pursue?' Tell you what, I am planning to pursue one fine male doctor today, so get your thoughts together and let's step out in style." I cancelled several hair appointments to accompany you to this function so start acting excited and introduce me to one of your male friends.

Georgetown Medical School Graduation Ceremony

To this, Krystal sharply responded, "You may be lucky today, because you may find your type in Dr. Smith." Dr Smith, that sounds good I can handle Mrs. Adele Smith very well.

They ended up staying for the entire ceremony.

Krystal was very surprised by the fact that many people were actually glad to see her, even to the point of asking for her contact information. Others teased her that she was looking for future clients. Most of the conversation was superficial and so she was very happy when Tamara wove through the crowd and hugged her from behind.

Yes, they did the usual girl stuff. They screamed, hugged and commented on each other's beauty, clothes and of course, dating. They almost forgot about Adele, who was more concerned about finding a date as she checked out each passing guy.

Finally, Adele could not contain her silence. "How come I don't see many brothers here? What type of brothers? Do you mean a religious brother, fraternity brothers or someone of your race? Krystal asked. "You know exactly what I mean; I was referring to a chocolate colored man. When is Howard University having their graduation? Maybe my 'type' transferred there," she added, and continued with her monologue. "All these kids already look rich. Do they need to be doctors as well? I guess the rich gets richer and the poor, poorer."

Tamara was very surprised by Adele's behavior and comment and even more so to find her in Krystal's company.

Adele and Krystal are not really cousins, but the Woods treated her like family. Her mother worked as a housekeeper for the Woods for many years and she brought Adele on weekends to work. The girls played well together and that was when Adele learned to braid hair by practicing on Krystal. When they started school in different school districts they grew distant and even further when Krystal went to college. Overtime Adele became very resentful of Krystal, her achievements and her "rich educated friends". Maybe she never liked the idea of her mother working as house help for another black family. Krystal was too busy to notice the change in her childhood friend so she continued to court her friendship.

Adele finally made eye contact with Krystal and Tamara, who had been staring at her as she talked to herself. "Why are you staring at me?" she asked. "Look at you two. You both look like models. What is the point in studying so hard to be doctors and lawyers? You can marry any of these rich guys any time."

As if they had rehearsed their response, Krystal and Tamara both said in unison, "We are able to support ourselves. We will marry for love and for love only."

"Dream on, dream girls. What does love got to do with this?" Adele replied.

Krystal added, "You are also beautiful, and an accomplished beautician. You must marry for love."

She responded sarcastically, "Excuse me, I am not a beautician but an excellent cosmetologist with subspecialty in hair transplant, or weaving as it is known in non-medical circles."

They all finally had a good laugh. Adele settled down in a lawn chair and the two friends tried to catch up on old times.

Tamara gave Krystal another hug saying, "Girl, I miss you. Why did we lose touch with each other?"

"I take full responsibility for that because I was trying so hard to put this whole place behind me," replied Krystal.

"Your cousin is so funny," Tamara added. "Why did she keep making references to her 'type'? She needs to take credit for her accomplishments."

"She was desperate to find a date so I promised to hook her up with Quarmaine." The girls had a good laugh at that, then Krystal continued "Oh if only she knew what a bad idea that would be. I wouldn't wish him on my worst enemy. Talking about Q, did he transfer to another school? I don't recall seeing or hearing his name among the graduates."

"Hmm, that is another story. He didn't transfer to another school, but he transferred to another facility," Tamara explained.

"What do you mean by another facility -like the psychiatric ward? Given his narcissistic personality, I knew he was crazy,"

"No, you are on the wrong path. Q wasn't crazy; he just had lots of family issues, which unfortunately landed him in jail."

"What!, prison- that is even worse?"

"Don't pretend to care, you never expected him to even graduate."

"Yes, I agree," she replied. "We said some mean things to each other. He was smart enough to graduate, but I could never envision him as a doctor. He was always angry about something, never showed an ounce of compassion. I could imagine him beating up his patients. I guess he could be an orthopedic surgeon. You know, break their bones and set them again." She started laughing while Tamara mustered a chuckle. "But seriously, I feel bad for him now. I hope he wasn't on drugs."

"No, Krystal, there you go again. It is far from that, but for now let us celebrate my graduation," said Tamara as she wisely changed the topic. "We need to have lunch this week, before I fly home. There is really so much to talk about, like this rock on my finger."

They screamed again like little girls, hugging and jumping, but they had to cut it short so Tamara could take family pictures.

Krystal and Adele also headed towards their car.

"I can't believe you had such fun after all your moaning and groaning. Do you still think you made the right decision in switching professions?"

"It is hard to say. I guess I could have done both. I couldn't stand anatomy, which is the study of the human body. It is almost impossible to become a doctor without anatomy. I also had a few minor issues with one boy in particular who considered me a distraction and a pretty dumb equivalent of a blonde," answered Krystal.

They both laughed at that blonde joke and wondered how anyone could have mistaken her for a "pretty dumb blonde girl."

"I don't see any difference between you and Tamara. She is just as cute and she made it through medical school. Why did you have to quit again?"

"Yes, Tamara is sharp, but she was more outgoing and more likeable. I just did not fit the mold, and Dad's position as an eminent board member and alumnus did not help either."

"Where was the brother you promised to introduce me to?"

"Oh, I'm sorry, you don't want to know. He got in trouble with the law,"answered Krystal. "I don't know the details. He had personality issues, but needless to say, it is still sad to see someone with such a potential waste away."

"That is what happens when a brother chooses Georgetown instead of Howard." If I had the opportunity to go to college I would have only gone to a historically black college like Howard or the other one in Atlanta, I can never remember the name.

"You need to change your mentality. We are free to go anywhere and be anything we choose. Yes, racism still exists in America, but that shouldn't be our excuse each time a brother gets into trouble. And secondly, I don't think we have to limit our education to only institutions where we dominate." 'The whole world is the Lord's and all humans created in God's image have authority to dominate and subdue this earth.'"

(Krystal really had strong opinions on certain issues, or perhaps on every topic.)

"When did you start getting religious?"

"I went to church with my grandmother last week. I daydreamed throughout the service, but the choir was very lively. None of the songs they sang were even in the hymn book."

Songs like "Overflow, he supplies all my needs, exceedingly abundantly, there is no room for much more, my cup runs over, thank you, Lord." (Nick Carter) "Lord, you are good and your mercy endures forever." (Israel Houghton)

By this time, they were almost home. Adele joked about going to church with the suit Krystal loaned her for the day but Krystal was quick to remind her that it was just for the day and not a gift. When they got home, Adele got in her car and left, while Krystal played with David, her mother's godchild whom she is in a process of adopting. She discussed her day with her parents over dinner and retired for bed.

THE TALE OF TWO BROTHERS

Many miles away from Georgetown, Q stayed awake in jail, overwhelmed with sorrow and confusion, not knowing if he would ever get his day in court; unsure whether or not he would ever become a doctor. The court appointed him a public defender since he couldn't afford a private one. He missed several electives and therefore was unable to walk through graduation with his class. This was the day he had lived for, the day that he would have been officially known as Dr Quarmaine Smith. As he lay awake he couldn't help but replay the encounters that brought him this low.

He had gone home to settle some issues with his brother, mainly regarding the prescriptions for controlled class drugs, which was brought to the Dean's attention. They bore Q's signature, written for several people in his neighborhood. He suspected his brother was responsible. Unfortunately, the meeting went very badly, bringing up old animosities and opening up very deep wounds. It was very obvious from their exchanges and demeaning comments that there were serious sibling rivalry issues which had never been dealt with. His brother saw him as the favorite and accomplished son, who considered himself much better and smarter. He had a horrible verbal exchange with him and it would have been physical had their mother not intervened. His brother left the house in anger and mistakenly took Q's jacket. They had both gotten similar jackets for Christmas.

Q left later and took the other jacket, without paying attention to the difference in its weight and threw it on his passenger seat. Fuming with anger, he went past the speed limit and the state police pulled him over. A routine search revealed cocaine, a loaded gun, and prescriptions bearing his name and signature. He denied ownership of the jacket and its contents, but could not explain why the name and signature on his driver's license matched the ones on the prescriptions. In his frustration, he even got physical with the police, ended up in jail that night, and has been there ever since. His brother refused to own up to his part of the crime, and has shown no remorse for what happened. He thought it was Q's turn to have some bad luck. In his attempt to punish Q and prolong police inquiry, he left home for a while and was later found overdosed on drugs and eventually admitted to ICU in a diabetic coma.

Quentin, his brother is only one year younger, who also had his hopes of playing professional basketball shattered like their father. He didn't just loose a father he lost his coach. Their father was really their pillar, as well as their part-time coach and motivator. He was the cohesive factor that brought the family together as one unit. During the latter part of his life, he went on disability and became like a stay-at-home parent, while their mother spent many evenings working third shift and overtime. He spent lots of quality time with the kids .He was a fun-loving dad until alcoholism and depression darkened his soul. He finally died from overwhelming sepsis after refusing to have his gangrenous foot amputated. Their mother went straight to work after their father's death to pay the bills, and the boys barely existed. Q buried his head in his books, thriving solely on his academic achievements and recognition. His brother on the other hand developed diabetes exactly a year after the painful death of their father. He was the youngest, and daddy's pet, so his diagnosis of diabetes intensified the blow of grief in his soul. To him, it was just a matter of time before he joined his hero in heaven. He slowly slipped into depression and became noncompliant with his diabetes therapy. It appeared that he was trying to hasten his trip to heaven. His kidneys began to fail, and the required dialysis only intensified the cycle of anger, frustration and depression, which led into drug use.

Q's mother and everyone in their neighborhood knew he was innocent but without the testimony and admission of Quentin, his innocence became difficult to prove. Quentin had been in and out of a coma with renal failure and declared incompetent to testify on many occasions. Q's emotions ran rampant, from anger to depression, but mainly anxiety, hopelessness and bewilderment.

He read the Bible through to help pass the time in prison, but it created more confusion and many unanswered questions. The chaplain had tried to reach out to him many times, but he could not comprehend why a good God would stand still while his life disintegrated. What purpose was this serving? He could not see what purpose was being served by his being in jail, or how it could work out for his good as suggested by some well-meaning preachers.

In his own mind, he was a good, hardworking person who has had his fair share of tragedy. He spent many hours reflecting on his career and what this time in prison would mean on his record. In the beginning, he even contemplated suicide, but the picture of his mother gave him reason to hold on.

In jail, Q made no friends, but when some inmates found out he was a medical student, they teased him constantly with their fake medical symptoms. However, the guards respected him and managed to get him some of his medical books so he could pass the time studying. He was even assigned to help in the clinic, where he kept his clinical skills updated. The clinic was more of a sanctuary as well, especially on days that Dr Jones covered. He really encouraged Q and never left without saying, "You are an excellent doctor and I know this place will soon be behind you, because help is coming from an unexpected source." Oh how true that statement was.

A Forgiving Heart

Krystal and Tamara met at a fancy Thai restaurant in D.C. to rekindle their friendship. Krystal could eat Thai food every day, her favorite being their crispy spring rolls, pineapple fried rice with some curry on the side.

They started with their usual giggles, and started their conversation on Tamara's upcoming wedding to Nicholas (Nick). They have dated since first year in medical school and he actually inspired their friendship. It was going to be in Atlanta in a few months and Tamara just couldn't wait to tie the knot.

Krystal was all ears and tears as Tamara described the wonderful love she shares with sweet Nick.

They ended their meal with sticky rice and mango slices for dessert.

Tamara mentioned her intention to visit Q before leaving for Atlanta in a few days.

Krystal was taken by surprise because she didn't think she would care for someone like Q. Tamara therefore proceeded to update her on the tragic life of Q without making an excuse for his treatment of Krystal in the anatomy lab.

She discussed how the attitude of the entire class towards him had changed once his life became an open case with the admission of his mother and brother to the hospital.

"He accepted my invitation to join our Christian fellowship and we have been good friends since."

It appeared that they were going to spend another hour after dessert talking about Q so Krystal ordered more spring rolls and sticky rice.

Tamara continued her story on Q by sharing his version of the incidence with his brother which eventually landed him in jail.

"With everything that I know now from studying medicine, the family would have benefited from family therapy."

Krystal sighed. "This is a world I have never known. I can't even imagine such tragedies, but how did Q manage to end up in medical school? I guess his friendship with his books paid off."

"Well, we didn't see the real Q before his father's death, but he really had taken on a strong personality to block the pain and focus on his dreams. He saw medicine as the only way to break the yoke of poverty and bad luck, 'the curse' as he calls it, over his family.

"Q's mother did not have enough money to post bail for him, so he has remained in jail awaiting his trial. Meanwhile, the case against him has become more complicated, since ballistics matched the gun he was carrying to one used to assault a police officer."

"This is unbelievable. This story has no ending. This is horrible," added Krystal, who could not believe the complexity of the story. Within minutes, her hatred for Q turned into great compassion. She finally inquired, "Why couldn't anyone come to Q's rescue? Why didn't the Dean help his favorite student?"

"He favored him because of his academic excellence, but his social life was still a mystery, and the case against him was gaining momentum each day. Remember, that was also the same day the Dean had interrogated him about the prescriptions, so it was really difficult to defend him. The cocaine, gun and traffic violation were beyond the Dean's influence, but he did acknowledge that he was an excellent and dependable medical student. Q's only hope now is for his brother to come out of his coma and come to his defense. His mother knows that Q is innocent, but how do you turn in one son in exchange for the other?

Krystal was deeply touched by his story so she promised to talk to her father, the prominent lawyer and member of the hospital board, about Q. The friends parted, and made another date to visit Q together.

Unsolicited Help

Krystal shared Q's story with her parents just as she promised wisely omitting their encounter in the anatomy lab.

Mr. Woods was equally touched and was very surprised that it had never come up for discussion at any of the board meetings.

Krystal managed to pull out some old class pictures that included Q, to help her parents familiarize themselves with him. Her father promised to follow up on the case. There was one condition though, and it was for Krystal to do all the groundwork, with a promise to join his practice in the future.

He ended the conversation by saying jokingly, "But if this happens to be a bad case, then your future is ruined to start with."

She answered, "No, Dad, not for working for the poor and innocent. My reward will always come from God." She was on a mission that would change her life forever.

Krystal had always lived for herself, but tonight she was convicted to help someone she did not even like.

"God," her dad retorted. "Did I hear you try to quote scriptures? Wow, what happened to my sassy little girl?

As the next day dawned, Krystal woke up in her comfortable bed, wondering what help she could give Q, while Q, who never slept, stared at the ceiling, wondering if help would ever come. Help was coming, but not as he would have expected. He had not seen nor thought of Krystal for more than three years, but Krystal never forgot him. Her memories of him were as vivid as the day she left medical school.

This overwhelming desire to help him was rather insane, but she couldn't shake it off. Q did not deserve a minute of her precious time, for so many reasons. In her reality, he was not in her social class, even as a classmate, and definitely not as a jailbird.

She finally got out of bed and prepared to meet with Tamara. The girls met as planned and drove together to see Q at the prison.

Q initially didn't recognize Krystal, but when Tamara introduced her as "Sophisticated Miss Krystal", he felt very uncomfortable and very embarrassed that she would see him in that state. His attitude made even Tamara very apologetic.

"Q, I am sorry for bringing Krystal along, I almost forgot all the drama you two had in first year. We had lunch together and I invited her along. By the way she just graduated from law school and interning with her father so she has a lot of time to do some research into your case. Q whispered to Tamara "No thanks I have my own lawyer, and besides she is yet to take her bar exams"

Q was still not very happy about Krystal's presence. "Why did you bring her, T? I don't need her unsolicited help. I can't afford her and I don't need her pity."

"Krystal is a very compassionate and sensitive person. We just never made the effort to really know her in med school."

He reluctantly acknowledged Krystal, while she wisely made herself invisible by turning her back to them. She became just a silent companion. Tamara continued encouraging Q not to give up hope. She intentionally referred to him as Dr. Q the entire visit. Q was teary as he remarked on his status; that his stint in jail would cloud his future practice, even if the whole world were aware of his innocence.

Tamara quoted her favorite scripture, "With God all things are possible," but this time his response was unusual as he mumbled, "What father would let his son suffer like this?"

Tamara responded, "First, Q, God did not orchestrate everything you have been through, but He can and will fix it in the long run."

"Well, His strategies are too complex and His timing very poor. If that's the way He plans to get my attention, then He has it. Why would God allow this to happen to me?" asked Q. "My whole life is disintegrating while He stands still."

Tamara tried to answer his questions by stating, "I think you are the one who needs to stand still and see His salvation. There is even a scripture to that effect and another in Psalm 46:10, which says, '**Be still and know that I am God.**'"

"Well, there is nothing to do here, shouldn't that qualify for stillness?" Q asked.

"No, being still is a state of mind and has nothing to do with activity," answered Tamara. "It means not to worry about things you cannot change, but trust in God."

"How, tell me how not to worry?" Before Q could say another word, tears flowed profusely down his face and onto his clothes.

Krystal could not believe how broken he was. She turned away while Tamara rubbed his hands and prayed for him.

As they prepared to leave, Krystal finally gathered enough courage and asked Q's permission to solicit her father's legal advice.

Surprisingly, Q rejected her offer, stating, "I really don't need your sympathy."

Krystal resisted him this time, but she still got in the last word.

"You are right, Q. You don't need sympathy, you need justice, and that is all I am offering." She turned to Tamara and whispered, "He has not changed one bit,"

They concluded their visit and left the premises after going through the routine security procedures. Tamara made a poor attempt to find an excuse for Q's bad behavior, but Krystal believed that Q was too proud to receive help. She concluded that even God could not help him, but Krystal was wrong. God, in His graciousness, wanted to help Q even though he was rude and undeserving.

Well, as disappointed as Krystal was that day, she still could not get Q out of her mind. She spent several days battling with the conviction that she had to help Q. She finally got too overwhelmed with this unusual compassion towards Q and begged God to remove the burden before she made a fool out of herself.

That prayer was not answered. Rather, her burden intensified, until one day she asked Adele to accompany her to the correction center.

SINCERE HELP

Krystal and Adele paid Q a visit and she discussed her commitment to help him. The visit was again short and very awkward for both of them. Q was more receptive but neither repentant nor appreciative. He still considered it an intrusion, but Krystal was committed to this good deed.

Adele questioned why Krystal desired to help. "He doesn't seem to appreciate your visit. The brother has a mean attitude. He is kind of cute, but I have had too much bad luck with men. I hope you are not trying to fix him for me." She chuckled. "Well, I guess a bad doctor is better anytime than all the men I have been with."

"Adele, can you for once in your life stop looking for men, how could you even think of a date in a place like this".

"Just for your education Miss Krystal, all the good men are behind bars"

They both laughed as they walked off, but Adele had more to say.

"Wait a minute, Krystal! You know what they say about enemies making great lovers. You never know, girl, but that will be a story for a great movie. What will the title be? 'Rich Girl Meets Poor Boy'? No! 'The Lawyer and the Ex-convict.' Maybe, 'Ghetto Meets Refined.'"

Krystal tried to stop her, but realized she was just having a good time at it.

Adele started to scream and dance to her own music. "This is it, yes, yes, yes. I am smart I am smart I am smart I am going to be rich. I have the perfect story for a movie entitled, '**Unequally yoked**' or '**Illegally yoked.**'"

"How did you come up with that brilliant title?" asked Krystal. "I thought that phrase was used only in the Bible for a union between a believer and a non-believer."

"Definitely," she replied. "You believe in the law, he doesn't believe in the law. You hate being a doctor, he loves to be a doctor — he just cannot do it from jail. You are clean and he is on drugs. He is poor, you are rich. I don't even want him, and I hope you fall for him, because I will definitely be filming '**Unequally Yoked**,' or better still, '**Illegally Yoked.**'"

Krystal stated, "You have to find another way of making money, because I will never fall for him, case closed."

Adele spent the night at the Woods's, and the girls happened to catch a portion of Bishop T.D. Jakes's Mega Fest on TV. Impressively, several prisons across the nation were connected by satellite. The girls noted the great number of incarcerated, handsome black men, and started a long discussion about the system, the waste of black male resources, the AIDS epidemic, the down-low epidemic (quietly gay), and why only 60 percent of black adults were married.

At the end of the show, both girls resolved that Q, like any other brother, deserved a second chance. They said a simple prayer for him, asking specifically that God would protect him from all that could happen in the jail and for God to direct good people into his life. They even asked God to shield him from physical, mental, and even sexual abuse, and from any incurable diseases. Their prayers flowed very easily out of their sincere hearts, just as if God Himself were praying through them. They ended with, "Even if he is guilty, please give him a second chance."

Adele was even moved to tears and was amazed at how Krystal's grandmother's voice rang through their prayers." I had to open my eyes because I thought she had joined in like an angel."

Krystal discussed her visit with Q with her dad before retiring to bed, and convinced him to take the case in spite of his reputation of being a high-profile lawyer. He finally took Krystal seriously. He also remembered his struggles as a young child and was convicted to take up the case at no charge.

GOD WORKS IN MYSTERIOUS WAYS

It seemed as though God was finally answering all those prayers. One of the inmates who came in a few months later recognized Q and was very surprised to find him there. He confided in the guards that there was no need for Q to be there, because he knew the family and actually did drugs with Q's brother. He had even benefited from some of the illegal prescriptions his brother wrote. He willingly offered to testify in Q's defense if necessary.

He added, "I know why I am here, but he is one of the promising brothers we have in the hood and there is no reason why he should be here, no way."

The guard took note of that and reported it in Q"s file.

About the same time, Q's mother, out of boredom and frustration, decided to give the house a thorough cleaning — and perhaps put it up for sale. That was when she found a note under her youngest son's bed, addressed to her. It was a confession from her younger son, written before he became seriously ill. He apologized for mistakenly taking Q's jacket, and for making him spend time in jail for his actions.

"...In a way, I wanted Q to experience a bit of my bad luck. I wanted him to also experience how it felt to have your dreams shattered, like losing a basketball scholarship and dropping out of college. He has not missed a beat since daddy's death, while I have become a diabetic with failed kidneys and no college degree or income. It seems I was born just to die like my dad. Since I may soon die, I don't think it is fair for you to lose Q, too. I thought I was punishing Q, but I am actually destroying all of us. I am sorry for my actions or inactions. Please forgive me.
Love,
Quentin.

His mother fell flat on her face, praising God for the evidence and weeping at the same time. Hope was rekindled again as she sang, "The sun will shine again." (writer unknown)

She could hardly sleep. Her dreams were so vivid as she relived her life with her husband. Those were very happy days with both kids playing basketball, him carrying them both after a good game, barbecues, and many family reunions at birthday parties. Then there were scenes of family hardships arising from his battle with diabetes and his subsequent demise.

Mom woke up early, exhausted from all the emotions she relived in her dreams. She went straight to her pastor and they both went to the jail to share the contents of Mike's letter with Q.

Q also shared how one of his brother's friends had confessed to a prison guard after an apparent encounter with God at one of the Bible studies. He then told his mom about Krystal's promise to help, and he managed to find her cell number for his mom to call.

Mom could not help but sing, "He is an on time God. Yes He is. He may not come when you want it, but He will be there on time." (By Dottie Peoples)

No one could have orchestrated all this at the same time except the Almighty God, who controls time and destiny.

His mom wasted no time calling Krystal. After thanking her profusely; she made an appointment to see her. As arranged, Krystal met Q's mom the next day.

Krystal was confident about the case now and could not wait to share these new developments with her father.

FREE AT LAST

Q finally got his day in court. There was so much evidence to support his innocence.

There was his brother's letter, the other inmate's confession, and Q's own good record.

Due to the overwhelming nature of the evidence, his case was dismissed. Everyone was jubilating, everyone except Q. He was in shock, emotionless. In just a moment, he had gone from despair behind bars to emptiness and hopelessness in the face of freedom.

For a long while his head was bowed, and then his tears began to flow. He could not even say thanks to his supporters. His mother filled the gap by giving Krystal and her father big hugs and drowning them with her tears of gratitude.

What was he thinking? He was definitely overwhelmed by the realities of his newly found freedom.

Q, his mother and a few of her church members went to their pastor's house to continue their celebration and to offer God His deserved praise and worship. The pastor's wife emptied her fridge and pantry and made them a sumptuous lunch. Q and his mother stayed longer for more encouraging word, and prayers.

The very next day, Q armed himself with a plan to take back his life. The first thing on his recovery plan was to meet with Krystal and her dad to express his sincerest gratitude, as well as offer an apology for his attitude in court. The next plan was to go back to the medical school to help set his records straight and to finish his degree.

Q called Krystal and arranged to meet her at her dad's firm, accompanied by his mom and their pastor. The office was a picture of luxury, of course, with nice portraits of the family on the walls. They greeted Krystal and her dad with sincere gratitude .His mom even knelt and wept before them as she demonstrated her appreciation. Q was also able to express his appreciation with a heartwarming speech. He was choking with tears and could hardly get the words out but he couldn't hold back his emotions. Facing the honorable Mr. Wood he said' "Sir, I am eternally grateful to you and your daughter for believing in my innocence and for sacrificing your reputation and time to represent an undeserving stranger like me. I have been so skeptical since my father's death and have blamed the whole world for all the painful changes in our family. This experience has opened my eyes to see that the world is still full of great people like you. Thank you for giving me another opportunity to hopefully get my medical degree."

He had more to say but his voice finally broke as he began to sob uncontrollably. His mother held him in her arms as their pastor rubbed his back. Krystal's dad was quick to direct all the credit to her, adding, "This was a great experience for Krystal and very rewarding, because it confirmed her passion for justice and her sensitivity to real life issues. We are all winners and I pray that you will get your life together and perhaps even get counseling to help deal with all the emotions that you haven't dealt with."

His pastor said, "Amen," and then added, "Child, forgive, forgive, forgive. You will be better for doing it. Forgive your dad for not taking care of his illness, your brother, the system and perhaps even yourself."

Q, still with tears in his eyes, asked Krystal to forgive him for judging her wrongly at med school. "That was prejudice. I may not be racist, but it is wrong to pass judgment on someone without fully knowing them. I was hateful to everyone and must have made your life miserable. Forgive me for our encounter at the anatomy lab and for every unpleasant encounter. I did not deserve your sympathy and I certainly did not deserve your kindness, but you showed me mercy. You're a better person than I could ever be, and for the first time in my life I acknowledge that I was an angry and proud Black man." He tried to show a dry sense of humor by saying, "Maybe I should write a memoir of my life entitled, 'Diaries of a Mad Black Man.' As much as I hated jail, in a way it humbled me. I never thought I would be the one to end up in jail. I wanted to be the perfect son and I stepped over my brother to do so."

He apologized to his mother as well and humbly asked each one to pray for him. The pastor seized the moment and prayed for everyone.

Krystal's dad ended their visit by giving them an open invitation to their Thanksgiving dinner.

THANKSGIVING DINNER — A GRATEFUL HEART

On Thanksgiving Day, Mrs. Smith had a lot to be thankful for. As has been the culture of her church, Thanksgiving Day starts with a service at their church. The whole service is dedicated to praise, worship and testimonies of God's goodness and faithfulness over the past year. The service started at 8am and ended at 10 am. Immediately after the service the sanctuary was transformed into a restaurant with the men setting up tables and chairs and the women serving pancakes and sausages to the homeless and any hungry member of the congregation.

Q participated wholeheartedly and helped even in the kitchen after the tables were set. He was so happy to be able to give back to the community and offer help to someone else in need.

In the past he was extremely critical of the homeless and complained that the church was encouraging irresponsible behaviors. They left church at 11.30 and got home just in time for mother to take out her turkey from the oven. Within an hour her home was filled with some church members and well wishing neighbors for a sumptuous lunch. She had to work in the evening so she couldn't accompany Q to the Wood's home for dinner but she made them her signature sweet potato pies.

At about 5 pm Q, still with a full stomach, set out for the Wood's home in a plush neighborhood in Mitchellville Maryland. He arrived at their door with a basket of pies, wine in one hand and roses in the other hand. The whole family was so excited to see him and quickly whisked the flowers placing them in a gorgeous vase. The pie became an immediate favorite at dinner. Q ate very little but made sure to try every dish on the table.

To break the ice, Krystal teased him, saying, "You cleaned up well, Q."

He really didn't know how to respond to her compliment. It took him by surprise and he became bashful.

After dinner, Q surprised Krystal's mother by offering to help with the dishes and all the trash.

Mr. Wood invited him to join the other men for coffee and to leave the ladies to finish in the kitchen.

With Q out of the way Krystal's funny mother teased her quietly. "I guess God just paid you back with a hard-working husband. God knows you need a domestic one, because you never stayed in the kitchen."

"No! No — no, Mom! You have no idea how mean he can be. I really don't know this fine-looking 'yes ma'am' man," answered Krystal.

"Precisely," replied Mom. "He is a new man."

"Mom, please stop that. Even Adele does not think he will fit into our refined culture. His past will taint my profession-The lawyer and the Ex-convict '!"

"I beg to think differently, my child. It is the lawyer and the doctor. If you thought he was guilty, why did you even bother to defend him?" Mom used that as an opportunity to advise Krystal. "In the first place, when did you start listening to Adele, anyway? Baby, if you think that your dad and I have always been rich and sophisticated, then please forgive us for lying to you. We have been so blessed that we have almost forgotten the struggles we both grew up with. We hated our lives of poverty so much that we worked hard to overcome it. We bought our parents homes in nice neighborhoods, thus cutting our ties with poverty forever. I have been judging myself lately, and have realized that some of my priorities have really changed. I have come to appreciate the true friends I had growing up as I evaluate all the superficial, rich acquaintances I have surrounded myself with.

"I am not saying you can't be rich and be a great person as well. Yes, you can. Look at you, Krystal. You have a big heart, so generous and so sincere. God bless the person who will take the time to reach beyond your outward beauty, your social status and your 'guts' to touch your soul. It is my prayer that you will learn to accept people for whom they are and not prejudge them, because that is the root of all prejudice. Krystal, my darling, do not build walls around you. Just enjoy life, love and laugh. I am not trying to start a relationship. You are gorgeous and men will always fall for you, but do not be impressed by only the rich and famous. Take time to develop true friendship. That will last even when the wrinkles overtake you."

They hugged, but Krystal, as always, had to have the last word: "No wrinkles, Mom, not in this era of Botox."

They both laughed and joined the rest of the party for coffee and desert.

Q asked to be dismissed said good-bye to the family and thanked them again for their hospitality.

Krystal would have remained seated, but her mother motioned her to see him off. As Krystal saw Q off, he extended his hand in friendship, asking her over and over for her eternal forgiveness.

"Krystal," he said, "I didn't even like myself. I poured my frustrations on everyone. If my meanness was what finally pushed you into becoming a lawyer, then I am glad for that, because you are a great lawyer. You were created for this profession. I may have been used by God to push you into your destiny."

Krystal smiled and said, "When did you become God's agent?"

"Seriously, I can never repay you for believing in someone like me. Someone who has nothing to offer, except perhaps do your dishes, polish your shoes, change oil in your car, pick up your dry cleaning –whatever you need please let me know and I will be honored to serve you. You do not have to be nice to me anymore, because you have done more than enough. I am free to dream again because of God's amazing

GRACE and the kindness of your family. By the way, you made the right decision to leave med school, because you are an amazing lawyer."

They laughed, hugged, and said good-bye.

A Season of Restoration

With his favorable verdict and a growing faith in God, Q returned to medical school after several meetings with the Dean. During his clinical rotations, he made a conscious effort to spend more time with his ailing brother.

He was able to forgive him and sincerely prayed daily for his recovery. He realized how much he had missed talking to him, as he did a lot of soul searching by his bedside. During one of those visits, his brother regained consciousness. His recovery was slow but progressive.

Q involved himself in every aspect of his care playing the roles of father and physician.

It seemed the whole family was getting on very well, and laughter was gradually restored to their home.

During this season of recovery, he began to make occasional calls to Krystal, who was always cordial and respectful. He made sure to always remind her of his availability to help her with her errands.

Krystal finally accepted Q's offers to help and asked him to escort her to a friend's wedding one day. He had some money now, and he also had a nice car, but not nice enough for Krystal, he thought, so he borrowed his friend's Mercedes for the occasion. He arrived at Krystal's house sharply dressed and even had on white gloves and a chauffeur's cap to complete the humor.

Krystal had a good laugh when she answered the doorbell and so did her entire family, when Q greeted them and said, "I am here to pick up Miss Daisy."

He opened the door for her and insisted that she sit in the back seat, and be chauffeured. He had a nice tray of snacks, chocolates and roses for her in the back.

Wow! Did he go all out! She thought.

Her mom watched them through her bedroom window, but David her soon-to be adopted little brother, pretending to say good-bye to his sister returned to tell their mom all the surprise treats on the back seat.

At the wedding ceremony, Krystal caught Q shedding a tear during the vows, and so she playfully said, "Are you okay? Or did someone leave you at the altar?"

He answered, "No. I have never been in a serious relationship, and listening to those vows makes me realize how empty my life really is. My main concern is that I do not think I deserve a commitment like that. I have nothing, absolutely nothing to give anyone."

Krystal tried to comfort him by timidly putting her arm around him, but he shook it off briskly, unintentionally hurting her feelings. He walked out even before the ceremony ended. Krystal was very embarrassed, thinking that Q might have taken her gesture wrongly. She was also concerned and upset about what the others might be thinking, but no one really noticed a thing between them.

That was stupid girl, stupid, what was I thinking when I took such an initiative of putting my arm around him? Oh my God, how humiliating it is to have him even think I like him, but much worse is to be rejected by someone I was never attracted to. Gosh, this is making me sick.

She sneaked to the restroom waited until the ceremony was over and mingled with the crowd, all the while trying to locate Q. She finally found him in the back seat of the car, still sobbing and praying.

She joined him and they sat in silence for a while before she gathered enough courage to ask, "Q, are you okay, or do you want to leave? We don't need to go to the reception."

He apologized to her. "I'm really sorry for messing up this beautiful day. I never saw it coming, but it is obvious that my life is still complicated. Even though I'm no longer in prison, I am still bound by my past and my soul is still imprisoned."

"I don't know what to say but you have come a long way and I believe you can overcome whatever it is you are feeling, too."

"Easier said than done, Krystal, because what I am feeling is love for you, but I can't love you or any woman the way you deserve to be loved, because I don't even feel like a man. My very manhood is lost."

"I hope you don't mean what I think you are saying. I mean, are you gay or 'down low,' whatever the new term is?" Krystal asked with much concern.

He surprised her when he said, "Truly, Krystal, I don't know what I am or who I am"

" Gosh, what do you mean by you do not know what you are? Give me a break. You are much smarter than that Q."

Q corrected himself. "Krystal, please, I am not gay, but I was robbed of my manhood in jail, I was raped, drugged and raped by idiots. Only God knows what I may be infected with. I have waited all my life for a moment like this, to fall in love and present myself pure to my bride, but I can't because I have nothing to give."

This was too much for Krystal. She made sure to remind him that nothing was going on between them. However, she was curious to know if he had ever had a girlfriend.

As far as she was concerned the mere fact of being raped shouldn't make one question their sexuality.

"Not really, Krystal," he responded. "I had opportunities, but I was too busy with school and taking care of my dad. Most importantly, I chose to preserve my love and affection for that special person. Truthfully, it was hard to find what I desired in my neighborhood."

"There is no one for you in my neighborhood either," Krystal interrupted. "We are just transitioning from enemies to friends and nothing more."

Q said with renewed seriousness, "I am not looking for a relationship. I really need help from someone bigger than myself. I have heard the message of salvation over and over. I have gone through the motions, but if I ever felt like being born again all over again, it is right now. I need to pour out my heart to God – if you don't mind, I would like to go back to the church alone while you talk to your friends."

Krystal did as he requested. Q went to the church and laid at the altar. He confessed everything, forgave everyone, and asked God to go to the deep recesses of his soul and cleanse him thoroughly; to give him a fresh start.

God certainly met him there. He had an experience that he still cannot formulate in words. He felt a presence so tangible that made him afraid to open his eyes least he saw God with his naked eyes. He felt a love so warm that he made his own vow to God just like the couple did-promising to love and serve Him the rest of his days on earth. A peace came over him that brought Philippians 4:6 to light — **"Be careful for nothing; but in everything by prayer and supplication with thanksgiving let your requests be made known unto God. And the peace of God which passes all understanding, shall keep your hearts and minds through Christ Jesus."**

Then as if someone was tickling him, he busted out laughing uncontrollably in the sanctuary. He would have laughed for hours if Krystal hadn't walked in. She stood and watched him for a while and she startled him when she began to laugh at him. Soon they were both laughing so hard they had to cover their mouths in order not to draw any attention from outside.

They enjoyed laughing so much that they almost missed the whole reception.

They left the sanctuary spent a short time at the reception and then rode to Krystal's paternal grandmother's house for some real soul food. Krystal had called her to request a special meal when Q was alone in the sanctuary. Krystal remained calm during the ride to her grandmother's. She still didn't understand what went on in the chapel and how Q's countenance was so transformed. She really needed to be alone with her grandmother to help her process all the information that Q had downloaded on her. How she had learned that her enemy/ex-convict friend may be in love with her, but that he could also be harboring a deadly disease like AIDS or hepatitis.

The silliest thing was that her heart was getting tender towards him. She was scared that she might fall for "this nightmare." She needed her grandmother's chicken soup and some "soul soup" as Granny called prayers and intercession).

As they rode, Krystal teased him, "You are like a new man Q. God surely chased those demons away. I would give anything to see a smile like that on your face any day."

"Are you for real, babe? Oh sorry, I meant Miss Daisy. Anything? What about marrying me one day?" Q asked jokingly. "I know I have a lot of work to do, but I will wait as long as you need me to."

Krystal had an answer for him, but Q forbade her to respond.

"Do not say anything yet. Let it be my figment. It will give me something to look forward to as I rehabilitate. Moreover, if you fall for someone, I would have still won by hoping for the best that God could ever offer. Until then, I am here for you, a work in progress and a recipient of His amazing grace."

When they arrived at her grandmother's doorstep, she welcomed them with a huge smile, as well as the sweet aroma of her cooking. "Granny" as she is affectionately called, liked Shirley Caesar and she had her music on – very loud, which depicted her usual disregard for her neighbors. The atmosphere was filled with the presence of God and there was that peace again that Q was getting accustomed to. They relaxed and enjoyed her southern cooking, but as everyone knew, nobody ate Granny's food for nothing. With dessert and tea came the "soul soup" — the counseling and the praying.... and more praying.

By the time they left, Q was ready to soar and Krystal was as supportive as could be. They both had a renewed faith in God and a peace knowing that He was in control of every aspect of their lives. They did not have to make anything happen; they just had to trust God, one second at a time.

Amazing Grace

Krystal and Q stayed in touch but soon their busy schedules and her travels made it impossible to build a true relationship. She always made time for him whenever he had a legal question. Q never forgot her birthday and sent her thoughtful cards regularly. His cards were always so appropriate it appeared as if someone was coaching him about how to emotionally connect with her.

He worked very hard and time seemed to have flown by. He finished all his clinical rotations, passed his boards, worked in the ER for a year, and then started a residency program in radiology. All this happened in just 2 years.

He also underwent thorough medical evaluation and tested negative for all the diseases he dreaded, like HIV, STDs, hepatitis, etc.

Another part of his recovery included several counseling sessions, by himself and with his mother and brother. He became active in church and made his salvation sure. He read every self-help book available, went to as many Christian men's meetings as possible, and kept himself pure from sexual immorality.

He bought a small house even as a resident in radiology and after his mother sold their old home he was able to accommodate her and his brother. He made peace with his brother and helped him cope well with diabetes. They all changed their eating habit and became great proponents of the "One Touch" glucometer and Stevia. Q was even able to convince one of the diabetic drug companies to feature his mother and brother in "One Touch" advertisements; another sure source of income for the family.

Q's brother resumed some courses online and started pursuing a degree in accounting at a near-by community college.

Things seemed to be going well. Sometimes it did not make sense. How their lives could go from chaos and uncertainty to peace and tranquility was amazing.

Certainly, God cared about the affairs of men. Yes, there was a time for everything according to Book of Ecclesiastes, and this was their season to enjoy God's goodness.

It was time for all the repressed feelings of love and affection to emerge. Q's life had been so complicated with family issues that he never allowed himself to fall in love, or perhaps he really could not afford to fall in love. Now he could. He could afford love; he had an income, he could buy roses and chocolates, but more importantly, he could give out love and actually even receive love.

He was beginning to take a second look at himself in the mirror these days, and enjoying all the simple things of life that once evaded him. Yes, it was the right time for him to start thinking seriously about Krystal again, since she constantly featured in his dreams. He had never followed up on his mock proposal because he felt unworthy then and even now. The thought of her always brought chills and tingling down his spine.

There was another member of Krystal's family that he was very fond of and that was her grandmother. That peace he felt at her house when he visited with Krystal kept drawing him till he made it a point to visit her every week. She became his main spiritual counselor and confidant. He would even buy her groceries and cook with her. She taught him how to pray and she also kept him updated about Krystal's schedules. Surprisingly they never visited at the same time but Krystal was aware of the special bond that had developed between Q and her grandmother.

Q knew he would have to confront the reality of his affection for Krystal one day, but right now, he was more comfortable with the figment of his imaginations.

He also had to wait for Granny to give him the green light when the time was ripe.

PERFECT LOVE

Krystal's "foolish heart," as she called it, was loving Q with each passing day, proving that "absence does makes the heart grow fonder," Q , may have been physically absent but he continued to send her cards and even started leaving her gifts at Granny's. In the meanwhile, she found herself in another relationship that looked perfect outwardly, but was simply mundane.

Fred, her new friend, was also a lawyer with good family roots. The problem was underneath his cultivated manner and impeccable grooming was the perverted mind of a person utterly devoid of moral scruples and integrity.

One day Krystal went over to Granny's to pour out the issues of her heart.

"Granny, she said, "Please, help me, because I am going crazy. I am in a perfect relationship and yet I think daily of someone with a prison record who may even have AIDS. Someone, who can be rude and obnoxious whose name, is as unprofessional as Q."

Granny absorbed it all with a grin and softly said, "Baby why don't you give him a call?"

She responded, "No way. He is the one who needs to be calling and thanking me daily for getting him out of trouble. He is the one who needs to be drooling all over me, because I am too good for him. Or am I? I feel awful. Why am I talking like this? I know better Granny. Why is my heart acting so stupidly? Why does it even want him?"

"I believe he wants you too, baby you are not the only one feeling this way. What did you think about all those cards and gifts"?

Granny held her to her bosom as Krystal sobbed and she prayed over her. She gently talked to her about God's perfect love, and how it made all men **equal**. How Jesus, the perfect and highest, gave His life for all people. According to the Apostle John in John 15; 13(NIV),

"Greater love has no one than this; to lay down one's life for one's friends."

True love was sacrificial, it knew neither class nor race, as Corinthians 13 beautifully described in the Amplified version of the Bible.

Granny picked up her Bible and they both read Corinthians chapter 13 aloud. Verses 4 and 5 really hit home as they both read, **"Love is patient and kind; love is not boastful, it is not arrogant or inflated with pride. It is not rude (unmannerly) and does not act unbecomingly. Love (God's love in us) does not insist on its own rights or its**

own way for it is not selfish; it not touchy or fretful or resentful; it takes no account of the evil done to it."

Krystal was enlightened by its content. She pondered on it and stated, "No one deserves to be loved like that, Granny. Did you love Grandpa like that? It would be nice to be loved like that, but I doubt if I can love anyone like that."

Granny took the opportunity to explain the scriptures. "You can, but only through Christ, because this kind of agape love only comes from God. That is how much God loves us. He can put that kind of love in our hearts. This kind is not just for our spouses, this is the God kind of love for everyone where no one is unworthy. That was how pure your love was as a child. You would cry each time you saw a homeless child and you always gave your toys away. We all change as we grow, and that is why we need to recommit our lives back to God for our own sakes."

With her head still on Granny's chest, Krystal rededicated her heart to God and asked Him for the grace to humble her heart to accept whatever His will was for her life.

Granny added a big "Amen," and with tears streaming down her face, she kissed Krystal's forehead. She said, "Oh, baby, this is the best thing you can ever do in your life. The rest is history. Your God has your best interests at heart. Oh yes He does. God has a great future for you, baby, according to Jeremiah 29; 11(NIV)

For I know the plans I have for you, declares the Lord, "plans to prosper you and not to harm you, plans to give you hope and a future"

Oh, how I pray for long life so I can see your expected end and the kind of husband He may have for you. Who knows, it may be someone entirely different from anyone you currently know. God knows exactly what you need because His ways are always higher than our ways. Yes, your friend Q has had many tragedies, but he is also a candidate for God's supernatural favor. Yes, he might not deserve you, but he deserves God's unconditional love as well. It does not have to come from you, but at least you can respect the fact that in spite of his background, tragedy, and shortcomings, he still managed to get his medical degree. That is a major accomplishment."

They ended their day with dinner, hot chocolate and "soul soup"

Boundless Love

Sleeping at Granny's on weekends eventually became Krystal's routine. They spent their weekends attending church and dining at fancy restaurants. They prayed each night for God's perfect will. Krystal was beginning to enjoy her new single, carefree life, until one evening an old friend driving through Granny's neighborhood decided to stop by.

Granny was beside herself when she answered her doorbell to find Q standing there wearing a huge, infectious smile. He didn't realize Krystal was visiting, and Granny had such fun surprising her. They rushed to hug each other like best friends, commenting on how stunning the other looked. Krystal appeared to be very comfortable with him.

Granny politely excused herself and only came out to serve them cookies, cakes, and iced tea. They chatted for a while and decided to drive around the neighborhood in Q's car in search of ice cream at a small café.

When he dropped her off, he had the courage to hold her hand and say, "Krystal, today was the best day of my life, please let us do this again, perhaps formally."

As usual, Krystal responded, "I hope you are not asking me on a date."

Before she could say any more, Granny interrupted and cunningly maneuvered Krystal to the kitchen with her, pretending to fix some goodies for Q to take home. She used that opportunity to remind Krystal of their prayers months ago, and advised her to give him a chance.

Well, she did give him a chance, as God did more with her leap of faith than she could have ever imagined.

Q regained his confidence as Krystal began to appreciate and show him due respect. They went on many dates and Q kept his promise to treat her like a queen, but more than that was the genuine respect and admiration he had for her. He adored her to the point that at times he would just stare at her in wonder.

They both committed to abstain from premarital sex, and any caressing beyond a hug or kiss on the cheeks. Q did everything right, but as Krystal melted into his arms with each hug, he knew he couldn't live another day without her.

He never let her out of his sight without promising, "Baby, I am going to make you the happiest woman on earth."

Krystal was always quick to correct him. "With God's help, you may."

With that said, he would pull her to him with his cheek against hers. With his eyes full of tears and throat clogged with emotions. He would say, "Baby, God has given me more than I deserve and I live to make Him proud."

With the help of his friend and mentor Dr. Agyeman, Q bought Krystal the most gorgeous diamond engagement ring. Dr. Agyeman, being African, was surprised to learn that he was just going to present the ring to her at a private dinner with no formal celebration or family.

Since he was the same friend who loaned Q his Mercedes on their first mock date, Dr. Agyeman, took credit for initiating their romance. He described their relationship as "Love brewed in an African's crib" He nominated himself as best man and instead of a bachelor's party for Q, he organized a proper African engagement ceremony for Krystal at his mansion a week before the wedding. He transformed his home into an African palace with traditional drummers and dancers and treated the guests to sumptuous Ghanaian and American dishes.

When everyone finally settled down, he offered a formal welcome and explained the purpose of the gathering.

"I met Dr Quarmaine Smith about three years ago when he worked briefly at my ER.

He bears such a strong resemblance to my younger brother that I started calling him Akwasi, my brother's name, and immediately adopted him into my family. Our bond grew even stronger when I learned his story and before long I found myself acting like his father and mentor.

As the adopted father of the groom, I want to thank the bride's family for raising such a treasure like Krystal and spending hundreds of thousands of dollar's educating her in the finest schools. I know this is unconventional, but since I have adopted Q, then as a father I have to honor Krystal as is expected in my culture.

A precious gem like Krystal deserves several kente clothes, bars of gold, cows, sheep, cocoa farms and everything that she desires. Can you imagine what King Solomon would have given Krystal had she been born in his kingdom?

Well Solomon is not here but Q is, so relax enjoy the meal and direct your attention to the big screen."

The video started with Q wearing elegant African attire with elaborate embroidery in a vast pasture with cows and sheep-it was hilarious. He greeted everyone and expressed his undying love for Krystal and how he was prepared to buy her all those animals but he thought she would prefer things from the mall instead.

The ensuing footage showed him running from one designer store to another and selecting gifts that covered everything that she would use in a day. He bought lingerie, sandals, bath gels, candles, perfumes, towels, finest sheets, jewelry, bags and even chinaware.

In addition, Dr Agyeman's brother who lives in London was also featured at Harold's Departmental store pretending to buy something but left with a bar of chocolate saying the stuff was not expensive enough.

At the end of the video presentation, the groom's party brought the beautifully wrapped gifts to Krystal and her family as they danced to the tune "let me cater to you"(By Destiny's Child). There were even gifts for Krystal's parents, her grandmother, and little David.

Dr Agyeman asked her if she would accept the gifts as presented. To everyone's surprise Krystal refused all the gifts, Q was confused and genuinely crushed not knowing that it was all part of the ceremony. The Agyeman's had coached Krystal well. So they asked her what would make her change her mind. That was when she demanded a bag of Hershey's kisses.

Her grandmother came to Q's rescue and pulled 3 big bags of Hershey's from her bag for him.

However Granny also refused to release them unless he planted a gentle kiss on her cheeks. When he attempted to kiss her the whole place erupted with jubilation as Krystal snatched those chocolates from her grandmother and asked Q to kiss her cheeks instead.

The Woods were very pleased and impressed with the entire ceremony. They found it very entertaining as well. They even danced to some African hi-life music before retiring home.

EVERLASTING LOVE

Q and Krystal's wedding day was spectacular and beyond anyone's imagination.

Yes, they expected elaborate décor and a reception befitting one of the most influential black families, but no one expected it to be so emotional and lovely. The guests shared tissue boxes as Q said his vows and the "elite" friends associated with Krystal's family who were initially consumed with prejudice against Q and his troubled past, left with much respect and admiration for him. Her parents' exuded pride as their colleagues commented on how blessed Krystal was and how they all wished their daughters could find such pure love.

Yes, it was pure; the purest that could ever be found, because it all came from Christ. It was not cheap love, because they both paid dearly for it.

Jesus died for such love, and Krystal risked her reputation and social class for such love. Q cultivated this love. Just like a decorated pumpkin, "Jack O'Lantern", he allowed Jesus to "scoop out" all the junk in his soul and replaced it with the light of God. God took his heart of stone, and like clay molded by the Master Himself, fashioned a love for His Krystal.

That night, many of the guests dreamed of Q holding Krystal's tearful face in his hands, and with his eyes looking as if he could see her heart he said, "My dearest Krystal, this day is all about you and my love for you. I do not need to hear you speak, just standing here beholding your face and your beauty means the world to me. If you should snap out of my dream world and walk out of here, I would be the first to applaud you, because heaven knows I do not deserve you, but God has molded my heart just for you and I really cannot help myself. You were raised with the best that life could offer, you really do not need me, but I need you. I need you to receive the love that is overflowing from my heart."

Krystal cried amidst the reception of his adornment and he continued, "I need you to wake up daily beside me, and I need your smile and your witty comments. Every breath you exhale vitalizes me. Thank you for taking a second look at me, because I am not the same person you met in medical school. I am a better doctor today because you accepted my love. I am a better person because God showed me mercy and gave me favor. I am a better person because He gave it all for me so I can also give it back to you. My prayer today and forever is for God to use me to meet every need of your heart, your soul and even body. I just want to be God's channel of blessing to you. I know as a fellow human being I can never replace God in your life, but God always uses people. I want to be the one He thinks of any time He chooses to bless you.

With God's help, I vow before all these people to love you and only you until death do us part; for better or for worse, in sickness or in health. I will, with His help, pray and fast as often as necessary to see you fulfill your divine destiny. I would like to have children with you one day. Yes, I cannot even wait to give you my first real kiss, but my favorite thing to do is what I am doing right now, right here, holding your flawless face, taking in your very breath and having your tears run on my fingers."

With that said, Krystal melted into his arms, and the pastor said "You may kiss your bride," even before they could exchange rings.

They may not have heard him say so, because they hugged for an eternity while the guests sniffed into their tissues. The minister then recollected himself and asked for their rings. They exchanged rings and then came the moment their guests had been waiting for.

"You may now kiss your bride."

Q gently lifted her veil back from her face, drew her again to his bosom, and planted the most affectionate kiss on her glossy lips, as live doves were released in the sanctuary with their favorite chorus in the background.

"My life will never be the same, my life will never be the same, my life it will never ever be the same," (by Juanita Bynum).

Their guests hung around and took many pictures of them as Q kept his focus on Krystal, totally oblivious to the guests. The happy couple had no time to pose for their pictures, but every moment was picture perfect. It was every photographer's dream.

They ate very little at their reception, but danced the night away after changing into comfortable clothes. They spent the first day of their honeymoon at a local resort before flying to Rome for a 14 night Mediterranean cruise. So as their guests were still dreaming about them, they spent the night not making love like most expected, but with Krystal soundly sleeping on Q's chest while he stayed awake, stroking her face and praying over her.

Coincidentally Q was not the only one awake and praying for Krystal.

Just before Mr. Wood fell asleep he saw an envelope addressed to him on his night table.

It contained a poem that Krystal had written for him entitled: "Daddy, don't forget me at the altar"

"Don't daddy; don't forget me at the altar
But go to the altar daily with me on your mind.
From birth till today, your arms have been my symbol of love, strength and comfort
But tonight I am resting in another man's arms experiencing a different kind of love which can never replace the unique bond we share.
Q also yearns for a father like you

So don't forget us at the altar but take us both daily to the altar and pray to the father above to help us all transition graciously.

Don't daddy don't cry at the altar but listen gently to the Father above as He whispers to you "Well done, thank you for showing your daughter the true heart of a father"

With tears streaming down his face he knelt before his bed and offered a simple prayer

"Help us God"

THE END